World Book, Inc.
180 North LaSalle Street
Suite 900
Chicago, Illinois 60601
USA

For information about other "True or False?" titles, as well as other World Book print and digital publications, please go to www.worldbook.com.

For information about other World Book publications, call 1-800-WORLDBK (967-5325).

For information about sales to schools and libraries, call 1-800-975-3250 (United States) or 1-800-837-5365 (Canada).

Library of Congress Cataloging-in-Publication Data for this volume has been applied for.

True or False?
ISBN: 978-0-7166-3725-7 (set, hc.)

Weird Food
ISBN: 978-0-7166-3734-9 (hc.)

Also available as:
ISBN: 978-0-7166-3744-8 (e-book)

Printed in China by Shenzhen Wing King Tong Paper Products Co., Ltd., Shenzhen, Guangdong
1st printing July 2018

Staff

Executive Committee

President
Jim O'Rourke

Vice President and
Editor in Chief
Paul A. Kobasa

Vice President, Finance
Donald D. Keller

Vice President, Marketing
Jean Lin

Vice President, International
Maksim Rutenberg

Vice President, Technology
Jason Dole

Director, Human Resources
Bev Ecker

Editorial

Director, New Print
Tom Evans

Writer
Jeff De La Rosa

Editor
Grace Guibert

Librarian
S. Thomas Richardson

Manager, Contracts and
Compliance
(Rights and Permissions)
Loranne K. Shields

Manager, Indexing Services
David Pofelski

Digital

Director, Digital Product
Development
Erika Meller

Digital Product Manager
Jonathan Wills

Manufacturing/Production

Manufacturing Manager
Anne Fritzinger

Production Specialist
Curley Hunter

Proofreader
Nathalie Strassheim

Graphics and Design

Senior Art Director
Tom Evans

Senior Visual
Communications Designer
Melanie Bender

Senior Designer
Isaiah Sheppard

Media Editor
Rosalia Bledsoe

TRUE OR FALSE?

WEIRD FOOD

WORLD BOOK

www.worldbook.com

TRUE OR FALSE?

A favorite Scottish dish—called haggis *(HAG ihs)*—is made by boiling a sheep's heart, liver, and lungs inside its stomach.

TRUE!

The chopped heart, liver, and lungs are mixed with oatmeal, chopped onions, fat, and seasonings. The mixture is then stuffed in a sheep's stomach and boiled. The cooked haggis looks a little like a fat sausage. Haggis is the national dish of Scotland.

**The Italians went crazy for pasta after
the explorer Marco Polo brought some
back from China in the 1200's.**

Historians say that people in what is now Italy had been enjoying pasta for hundreds of years before Polo's famous journey. Many scholars think that Italians learned to make pasta from a people called the Arabs.

TRUE OR FALSE?

An Asian fruit called the durian
(DUR ee uhn) stinks so bad that eating
it is not allowed in some places.

The durian is a prickly fruit about the size of a basketball. The flesh inside is sweet. But to some people it smells like sewage, throw-up, or what a skunk sprays! Some hotels and other public places have banned eating durian because of its smell.

TRUE OR FALSE?

The main ingredient in one of the world's most expensive soups is a bird's nest.

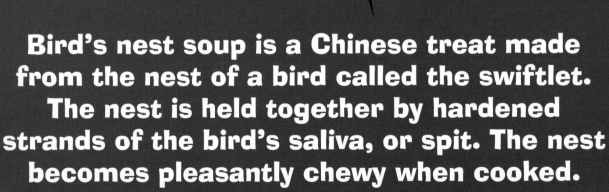

TRUE!

Bird's nest soup is a Chinese treat made from the nest of a bird called the swiftlet. The nest is held together by hardened strands of the bird's saliva, or spit. The nest becomes pleasantly chewy when cooked.

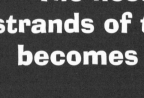

Celery is so hard to digest that you burn calories just by eating it.

Celery is a good low-calorie snack,
but you still get about 6 calories
for each stalk you eat.

TRUE OR FALSE?

Eating a certain kind of "miracle berry" before eating sour foods makes the sour foods taste sweet.

The miracle berry grows in west Africa. When people chew on the berry, it gives off a chemical that changes what their taste buds taste from sour to sweet. Even lemons and hot sauce turn sweet!

TRUE OR FALSE?

When the Greek flaming cheese dish called saganaki is brought to the table, diners may shout "Opa!" In Greek, this means "Call the fire department!"

Diners may shout "Opa!"
when being served a flaming
saganaki, but the word is simply
a Greek cry of celebration.

Bacteria are those "bugs" that can make you sick. Foodmakers try to avoid bacteria entirely because they spoil food.

Some bacteria do spoil food. But others make food. Yogurt, for example, is made using bacteria. The bacteria ferment (break down) chemicals in milk, turning it into creamy, tangy yogurt.

TRUE OR FALSE?

The dish hakarl, from Iceland, is made by burying a shark in the sand for several weeks.

The kind of shark used to make hakarl is full of a chemical called ammonia. Ammonia smells bad and tastes terrible. After it is caught, the shark is left in the ground for several weeks while bacteria ferment (break down) the ammonia. Then the shark meat is hung to dry for several months.

TRUE OR FALSE?

Thousands of people gather in Buñol *(boon YOHL)*, Spain, every year to throw tomatoes at each other in a giant food fight.

The food fight, called La Tomatina, happens on the last Wednesday in August. After the hour-long fight, the food fighters and the town square are covered in a slimy, red mess of crushed tomato.

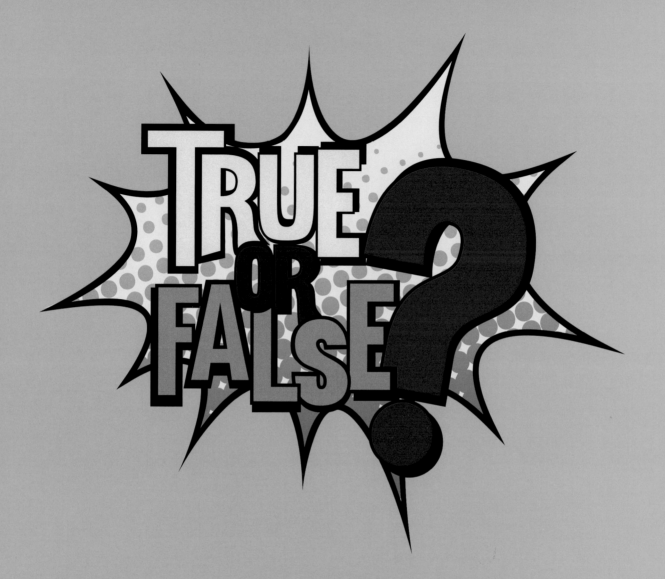

The potato comes from Ireland.

Potatoes are an important part of Irish cooking, but the potato came from the Andes Mountains of South America. Spanish explorers brought potatoes back to Europe in the 1500's.

Aboriginal people of Australia snack on a kind of ant called the honey ant for its sweet taste.

49

Honey ants have a special way of storing their food. Some honey ants are living food storage containers. They keep a sugary liquid inside their bodies. Dug up and popped in the mouth, these ants make a sweet treat.

Pineapples grow on pine trees.

Pineapples grow on a tropical ground plant that has long, spiky leaves. They are probably called pineapples because European explorers thought the fruit looked like pine cones.

pavlova

People in Australia and
New Zealand enjoy a fluffy white
dessert called pavlova *(pav LOH vuh)*.

Pavlova is a meringue (sweetened, whipped, and baked egg whites) topped with fresh fruit and whipped cream. It looks a bit like a tutu (ballet skirt) and was named for the Russian ballerina Anna Pavlova.

TRUE OR FALSE?

The world's hottest chili pepper is known as the Frisco face-melter.

**Frisco
face-melter**

The Frisco face-melter is fake, but there are plenty of fiery chili peppers with funny names. One of the hottest is the Carolina reaper. It's more than 300 times hotter than an ordinary jalapeño.

Carolina reaper

Some Chinese people enjoy a snack called "stinky tofu."

Tofu is a creamy white food made from soybeans. Stinky tofu has been "improved" through fermentation (breaking down) by bacteria. The result is a pleasant flavor but a strong, bad odor.

Sushi *(SOO shee)* is a Japanese food
that often includes raw (uncooked) fish.

TRUE!

Sushi is seasoned rice topped with other ingredients. Many people enjoy raw fish sushi, though it can also be made with vegetables, cooked seafood, or egg.

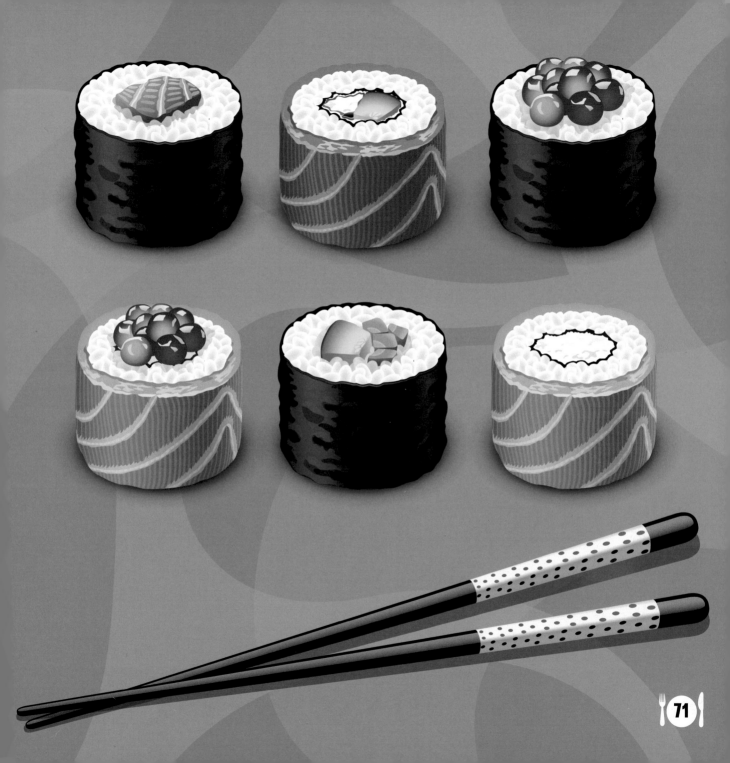

TRUE OR FALSE?

The sandwich is named after its inventor, the American country singer Johnny Sandwich.

What we today call a sandwich was probably invented in the 1700's by a British man named John Montagu. He was a nobleman whose title was Earl of Sandwich. His servants would bring him a slice of meat between slices of bread to eat when he was busy.

TRUE OR FALSE?

The ancient Aztecs liked to drink hot chocolate spiced with peppers.

The Aztecs loved chocolate. But it wasn't sweet! The Aztecs enjoyed chocolate as a hot, bitter drink flavored with chili powder and other spices.

For much of human history, adults have not been able to drink milk.

In nature, milk is a drink for babies. As human beings grow up, their bodies become less able to break down the lactose, or milk sugar, in milk. Today, many grown-ups can break down lactose. This is because of a genetic mutation (change in genes) that began to spread among human beings about 12,000 years ago.

TRUE OR FALSE?

The French dish escargot *(ehs kar GOH)* is made from steamed clams.

Escargot is made of cooked snails.

People in southern Africa enjoy
a treat of dried meat called biltong.

Biltong is meat that has been cured (preserved) through drying and salting. It may be beef or something more exotic, such as ostrich or wildebeest.

DID YOU KNOW...

Blue cheese

is prized for the dark spots and streaks of

mold

it contains.

According to folklore, garlic can be used to **repel vampires.**

Cabbage, broccoli, cauliflower, and Brussels sprouts all come from different varieties of a

single plant.

Koreans enjoy hundreds of different kinds of **kimchi**—spicy pickled vegetables.

The wild ancestor of the **banana** is a tiny fruit packed with hard seeds.

Poke *(POH kay)* is a traditional Hawaiian salad made with **raw fish.**

Index

Acknowledgments

Cover: © Guaxinim/Shutterstock; © Lapina/Shutterstock;
© Ded Mazay, Shutterstock

5-20 © Shutterstock

23 © JBryson/iStockphoto

25-27 © Shutterstock

28-29 © Jim West, Alamy Images

30-49 © Shutterstock

51 Public Domain

53-63 © Shutterstock

65 © iStockphoto

67-73 © Shutterstock

75 *Portrait of John Montagu, 4th Earl of Sandwich* (1783), oil on canvas by Thomas Gainsborough; National Maritime Museum; © Shutterstock

76-93 © Shutterstock